PERSEVERANCE
AND PERSISTENCE

LEONARD SANDBERG'S BIOGRAPHY

MARILYN SANDBERG GRENAT

PERSEVERANCE AND PERSISTENCE
LEONARD SANDBERG'S BIOGRAPHY

Scripture quotations marked TLB are taken from The Living Bible copyright © 1971. Used by permission of Tyndale House Publishers, Inc., Carol Stream, Illinois 60188. All rights reserved.

iUniverse books may be ordered through booksellers or by contacting:

iUniverse
1663 Liberty Drive
Bloomington, IN 47403
www.iuniverse.com
844-349-9409

Because of the dynamic nature of the Internet, any web addresses or links contained in this book may have changed since publication and may no longer be valid. The views expressed in this work are solely those of the author and do not necessarily reflect the views of the publisher, and the publisher hereby disclaims any responsibility for them.

Any people depicted in stock imagery provided by Getty Images are models, and such images are being used for illustrative purposes only. Certain stock imagery © Getty Images.

ISBN: 978-1-6632-1552-9 (sc)
ISBN: 978-1-6632-1551-2 (hc)
ISBN: 978-1-6632-1555-0 (e)

Library of Congress Control Number: 2020925807

Print information available on the last page.

iUniverse rev. date: 01/06/2021

Dedication

I dedicate this book to my children:
Annette and Dave, Jeff and Joanna, Kristina and John, and Jennifer and Bob.
And to my grandchildren:Owen and Paige,
Kelsey, Brett and Harrison,
Emily and Jeff, and Corrine.
And to my brother: Ralph E. Sandberg.

This story is about their Swedish immigrant
father and grandfather, Nils Patrick Lennart
(Leonard) Sandberg, and this is one of my
legaciesI am leaving with them, so they
will know from where their heritage
comes.

Lovingly, your mother, mormor
(momo), and sister,

By Marilyn Sandberg Grenat

Acknowledgements

I want to thank my dad for taking the time to tell me some cute stories of his past and for teaching me how to live in a sometimes unruly world.

He and mother were Christian parents who provided a solid, stable home and life-style for my brother and me in which to live.

Through my ups and downs of life my four children gave me reason to continue trying to live that way for them. I have been blessed with a good family and friends that always encourage me to write this story. I am just sorry it's taken me so long and that I didn't get it completed before my father passed. Even our Swedish relatives have been encouraging and anxious to read it. Sorry Swedish cousins, I'm not writing it in Swedish.

Thanks to IUniverse for believing in me to write one or two more books. My first was a poetry book called "Inspirations from the Heart", that was published on July 12, 2018.

Fondly, Marilyn Sandberg Grenat

Contents

Chapter 1   The Life of a Blacksmith..1

Chapter 2   Time at Laura Kristina's..9

Chapter 3   Nils' Adventures 15

Chapter 4   The Wonder of Today's Manfacturing 19

Chapter 5   More of Nils' Adventures...23

Chapter 6   Language lessons & The Swanson Family...................27

Chapter 7   A Little History of the Era & Lessons Learned 29

Chapter 8   Places Leonard worked & Marriage to Helen.............33

Chapter 9   Family Life in Peoria, Illinois...................................37

Chapter 10   The 1946 Family Trip to Sweden...............................41

Chapter 11   Back Home Again in Indiana & White Cottage Days ...49

Chapter 12   Leonard & Marilyn"s 1954 Trip To Sweden................55

Chapter 13   Back Home...59

Chapter 14   The 1960 Trip to Europe-First by Plane For
             Helen, Leonard & Marilyn 63

Chapter 15   The Family Grew..67

Chapter 16   Dad & Ann's Final Swedish Christmas Trip with
             Marilyn in 1992..71

Chapter 17   Final Time With Ann...75

Epigraph/Purpose

The whole purpose of this book is to leave a story of the man and others who started our roots for the purpose of teaching those who follow me. Our ethnic traditions and principals are to be valued and admired. I'm very proud of my father and what he stood for and accomplished in the New World.

Foreword

Marilyn Sandberg Grenat has provided an insightful biographical look at the life of a Swedish immigrant, her father, who was born in Sweden just over a century ago. Nils Lennart (Leonard) Patrick Sandberg spent his youth in Sweden, but left home for the USA in the mid-1920's. His life spanned the industrial revolution, the great depression, the atomic era, and the space age. Through all of these periods we learn how Leonard Sandberg displays the characteristics of perseverance and persistence to survive and excel in his adopted land.

I first met Leonard Sandberg when I moved to Lafayette, Indiana, in 1959. At that time, he and his wife, Helen, were active members of the church described in this book as the old Swedish Mission Covenant Church at 16th and Grove Streets in Lafayette. Leonard was in his mid-50's at that time while my wife and I were a young couple with a two-week old daughter. My first impression was that Leonard was a friendly "old" Swede with a heavy accent. That did not bother me at all since my own mother, like Leonard, had immigrated from Europe (The Netherlands) in the 1920's and had a noticeable Germanic/Dutch accent. When I first moved to Lafayette, Marilyn Sandberg was just finishing her college years at North Park College. Shortly after we moved to Lafayette, we ourselves became active in what came to be called the Evangelical Covenant Church of Lafayette. Our friendship with Marilyn has continued over the many years since, and we have come to appreciate her and her extended family throughout the many seasons of our lives. Because my main interactions with Leonard were primarily through church activities, I saw him mainly as a pillar of the church who by personal example demonstrated leadership and love to us younger individuals and families in the church. There were many details of his early life that I was unaware of until I had the opportunity to read some of the stories that Marilyn relates in this book. I found them to be fascinating. In particular, the descriptions of village life in Sweden, Swedish meals, Swedish homes, and customs will be of great interest to the reader. Further, the challenges faced by Leonard in America, and by many immigrants of that time, give the reader a better appreciation of the courage and resourcefulness it took to survive and to flourish.

Steve and Veva Swanson, relatives of Leonard who are mentioned in the book, were also active members of the Lafayette Mission Covenant Church and I was privileged to enjoy their friendship over the years as well. When Leonard's son, Ralph, (Marilyn's brother) completed his military service, I had the opportunity to meet and interact with him and his wife on their many visits to the Sandberg family in Lafayette. In reviewing the details presented in these stories about Leonard, I noted several coincidental events in our lives that seemed almost to cross paths in unexpected ways. Leonard's marriage to Helen, on June 29, 1935, occurred one day after the day of my birth. Who could have guessed that some 85 years later, I would be writing a Foreword to a book about him? Leonard's professional career included work at Ross Gear and at a Caterpillar facility in Peoria, Illinois. Years later, one of my daughters, who received her engineering degree from Purdue University, worked at both of those companies and locations.

My personal heritage is Dutch-German. However, beginning in 1959 with my introduction to the Sandbergs, the Swansons, the Larsons, the Swedish Mission Covenant Church, several pastors of the church who had Swedish lineages(Norbert Johnson, Goete Bringerud, Henry Johanson, Don Johnson), I soon began to appreciate and love the Swedish foods, the Swedish hymns, and other Swedish influences in our lives. In the Spring of 1964, Karl Osson, who was the President of North Park College during the years when Marilyn Sandberg was a student there, spent a weekend visiting and teaching at the Lafayette Evangelical Covenant Church. My wife and I were privileged to be his hosts for the weekend. Thus began our longtime association with North Park College where one of my own daughters eventually completed her college degree. Over the years my wife and I have enjoyed many a Santa Lucia celebration hosted by Marilyn Sandberg Grenat, thanks to the traditions passed on by Leonard Sandberg and his family.

One final note: A number of Swedish hymns that were initially new to me have become some of my favorites. One of them, "Tryggare Kan Ingen Vara" (Children of the Heavenly Father), was the traditional closing number for the North Park College Choir. Our Lafayette Covenant Church Choir sang it in Swedish at a city-wide choral festival one year, thanks to Marilyn's assistance in helping us correctly pronounce the Swedish words. That has reminded me once again that Nils Lennart Sandberg was one of those special "Children of the Heavenly Father". Thank you Marilyn Sandberg Grenat for sharing his story.

Dr. Paul L. Ziemer
Professor Emeritus, Purdue University
West Lafayette, Indiana

Introduction

This story has been a long time in the making. I have meant to tell this immigration story of my father for many years, but a busy life kind of got in the way. I would not have been able to complete it too early anyway, as my father lived to be a nice ripe age of ninety. However, it would have been nice for him to have been able to critique it for me. Sadly, he left me a few pages that I have carelessly misplaced, but my memory is still pretty good to remember many stories he told me in person.

I was always very proud of my Daddy and felt his magnificent story needed to be told. He was a self-made man with great entrepreneurship. He accomplished what he came to achieve, and he executed and attained it beautifully.

Listen, learn and enjoy family and friends for I hope you will perhaps not only learn fromhim, but perhaps gain a chuckle here and there.

Your loving daughter, sincerely,
Marilyn Sandberg Grenat

KLAS MAGNUS SANDBERG – 80 YEARS OLD

HAURIDA'S BLACKSMITH FARRIER

Chapter 1

THE LIFE OF A BLACKSMITH

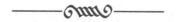

The village Blacksmith from a small village in Sweden wanted to teach his boys the value of learning a trade well worth their time. No matter what they finally choose to do, he wanted them to persevere and persist at doing their best. It didn't matter if they went to college or trained for a profession or trade they might finally choose. He wanted them to be thorough and do their best at whatever they chose. It was the Swedish way, and certainly the way of the Sandbergs. Klas Magnus Sandberg encouraged his Boys to succeed in their choices.

There once was a saying that, "That was a dumb Swede!" No, the Swedes were not dumb, but it was said by some lazy person who thought the Swedes were dumb for not taking shortcuts and being sloven in their workmanship. They most always wanted to take their time and do a good proficient job at everything they tackled.

One should be proud of their work and accomplishments. It is biblical.

I Timothy 6:1b says "Never let it be said that Christ's people are poor workers." I Timothy 6:10a says "The love of money is the first step toward all kinds of sin." I Timothy 6:6 "You are rich if you are happy and good." and I Timothy 6:17b says "Your pride and trust should be in the living God who always richly gives us all we need for our enjoyment."

The small village of Haurida, Sweden was bustling this cold crisp winter morning- especially around the Blacksmith shop.

Clip, clop, clip, clop. "Whoa-oa! Hej!" klas, "How's it going today?" "(Hur går det idag?)" bang,bang, clang! Yes, it's going fine today (Ja, det går bra.) I can't complain. I've got my two boys helping today and they've always got something to learn. My oldest boy, Georg, is always trying to invent something new. He's got the crazy (tokig) idea that he can make a machine that washes the dishes automatically. Is that farfetched or what? He's been learning how to solder stainless steel together, so guess my blacksmith shop has been a good learning ground for him.

My youngest, Nils Lennart (Leonard) has been learning how to forge tools.

While making horseshoes is prominent now, I don't know how much longer they will be needed. There are so many more technical things today with different properties, materials and procedures.

Horseshoes can be made of many different things. Steel nailed into the hoof wall, the palmar, of the hooves is what they do today and it's metal and sometimes partially made of synthetic materials that's designed to protect the hoof from wear. The palmar of the hooves is an insensitive hoof wall that is anatomically akin to the human toenail, only much larger and thicker. Early Asian Hipposandal (hoof boot) was put on working animals that were exposed to many conditions. They sometimes were wrapped in rawhide or leather which Romans attempted to use to protect their horses' feet with a strap of hipposandal, which was a predecessor to the horseshoe.

Since iron was a valuable commodity, the worn out items could be reforged and reused.

In 1897 four bronze horseshoes with nail holes were found in an Etuscan tomb dated around 400 B.C. Horseshoes with nails of the 5th century were found in the tomb of the Frankisah King Childeric in Tournai, Belgium.

About 1000 A.D. cast bronze horseshoes became common in Europe. Due to the value of iron, horseshoes were even accepted in lieu of coins to pay taxes. Hot shoeing, the process of shaping a heated horseshoe immediately before placing it on the horse, became common in the 16th century. Since the fitting of horseshoes is a professional occupation, conducted by a farrier, who specializes in preparation of feet fitting appropriate shoes. Some countries legally restrict this profession to people with specific qualifications and experience. In the United States, professional organizations provide certification programs.

Different materials can be used for different purposes like farmers, pioneers, polo events, show jumping, and western riding events. They needed strength and hardware, so they used steel. Lighter materials like rubber, plastic, magnesium, titanium, or copper have been used. Since aluminum shoes are lighter, they are used in horse racing.

People hang horseshoes over their door ways for good luck. With the ends pointing up it is considered a storage container for any good luck that happens to be floating by. To hang it upside down, is bad luck, as all the good luck will fall out.

Northern Europe, where the domesticated horses arose to it's modern form of horseshoeing because they were brought to colder and wetter areas than their ancestral habitats. Softer and heavier soils softens the hooves and make them prone to splitting, making hoof protection necessary. The domesticated horses must carry or pull additional weight. Irrigated land or urine in stalls can soften the horses' hooves. It's capsule is mostly made from keratin, a protein, that is weakened by exposure, which can make them more fragile and soft. A good farrier or blacksmith can create a corrective shoe with a proper shape, weight and thickness to help protect and correct the gait of the horse when there is added weight and stress of a rider, pack load, cart, or wagon. So don't, by any means, think this job is minimal. He must have a great deal of knowledge-much like a Podiatrist Doctor who can make corrective custom shoes to even help it's bone and musculature problems in their legs. No wonder their training is extensive and appreciated.

When hot shoeing is done, the metal is softened so that it can be more precisely shaped to the horse's hoof. The coals must be a certain temperature to make the steel malable not only for horseshoes, but other steel products like carts, buggies, and wagon tongues. Horseshoes can have studs added with Borium and Carbide-tipped road nails for traction on ice or muddy or slick conditions. A good farrier will remove the old shoe with pinchers (shoe pullers) and trim the hoof wall to the desired length with nippers, a sharp pliers-like tool, and then trim the sole and frog of the hoof with a hoof knife. If the excess hoof is not trimmed, the bones can become misaligned, which could place stress on the legs of the horse. Hot shoeing is more time consuming, but provides a better fit. Hot shoes are cooled in water before the farrier nails the shoes on and uses a rasp (large file) to smooth the edge where it meets the shoe.

Since skill, and experience and endurance are all important for the expertise of a good farrier, it is important to choose the very best for the best shoeing of your horse for his/your need. If Farrier is part of the Blacksmith's title, it implies he is a "Professional" horse shoer with skill, education, and training. An untrained, unskilled horse shoer can cause a lot of damage.

Our Farfar (Father's father), Klas Magnus Sandberg, was a true Farrier, that people for miles around Haurida, Huskvarna, and Jönköping relied on him to service their horses, wagons and buggies. His profession was skilled and admired.

"Do you need anything more today other than shoeing the horse (hästan)?" "You might check the buggy tongue (tungan) for me. It seemed a bit loose. I don't want the Mrs. (Fru) to have any accidents when she drives to market."

Bang, bang, clang. "Georg, make sure that fire is hot enough before you form that hot shoe to Herr (Mr.) Anderson's horse!" "Ok, Pappa, kan göra (can do)!"

Their sweet little yellow cottage (stuga) has three main rooms. A comfy kitchen with lots of warmth where good food is made with lots of love and good tastes and loads of good aromas, a stately, modestly formal living room, and one bedroom (sov rum). The kitchen has a long kitchen sofa, that can be made into a bed, under a double window, a water counter where there is always a full pail of cold drinking water from the well with a dipper, and a spacious woodburning stove where Laura Kristina bakes her delicious delicacies. The water kettle and coffee pot are always on the back of the large woodstove surface. There's always plenty of warmth in the kitchen as there is always a continuous slow fire going in the belly of the stove.

Laura Kristina had busied herself with her household chores all morning. She had limpa rye bread rising on the back of the wood cookstove. She had done up the morning breakfast dishes, and Klas Magnus, her blacksmith husband, was down at the blacksmith shop shoeing the neighbor Anderson's horses. He wanted to get them ready to pull the sleigh in the snow. Spring plowing would be upon them soon too, and all the plows had to be made ready as well. Klas would be wanting lunch soon. She wanted the first loaf of limpa finished before lunch, so she could make his favorite smörgås (sandwich) with limpa, butter, medvorst (similar to salami), and bond ost (farmer's cheese). This is a solid, sturdy, yummy sandwich made to truly make a man happy and full.

She also had made blåbär's kräm (cooked blueberry crème for dessert with lots of whipped cream for a topping.

The kitchen was filled with the lovely aromatic smells of the sweet limpa rye bread that had been baking all morning long. Laura found herself humming as she placed the pretty blue and white luncheon dishes on the table. She remembered the times when there were six of them around the table when all of the children were home. However she thought there would only be three of them today. She and her husband with their youngest, Nils, would get to share a rare lunch together this day. Nils had been down at the shop with his pappa helping out since he had been home from the Navy.

Laura brushed away a small tear of joy as she anticipated Nil's soon to be trip to the U.S.A. No other person in their family had ever wanted to venture out to so far away before. Laura Kristina was very proud of Nils Lennart's desire to better himself in the "New World". After all, did not folks say it was a land with "golden streets "? figuratively speaking, of course. It was to be a time of opportunity, and no one in their family had ever wanted to venture out that much before. Nils requested early dismissal from the Royal Swedish Navy to take off on his venture and the King of Sweden had to give this permission. He was happy he was getting to spend A few days at home with the folks before he had to leave to catch the Swedish/ American Line ship called the Drottningholm from Guthenberg (Göteborg).

She had a few minutes before the guys would be coming home, so she sat in her rocking chair to do a little more knitting on the woolen undershirt she was making for Nils to wear on his cold crossing to New York City to keep him warm. He would be arriving in February of 1926. Perhaps after supper she could finish it for him.

LEONARD AND HIS SPONSORS OF LAFAYETTE, IN.
CARL & ELEANOR CARLSON
LEONARD & CARL- 1926
ALGOT & SELMA SWANSON
5-12-40
MOTHER'S DAY
1941 LAFAYETTE, IN.
MARILYN AND GRANDMA AND GRANDPA SWANSON

Chapter 2

TIME AT LAURA KRISTINA'S

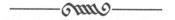

"Laura Kristina, I am home (jag är hem-ma)! Is Lunch ready? (Är mattan färdig?) We are really hungry. The boys and I have had a full morning of work at the Blacksmith shop (Smedbyn). I brought Georg and Ole home with me too for lunch." Even though Georg and Edit are married and live down the road, he comes at times to help his dad in the shop, so Klas Magnus likes to treat him to lunch, and Laura Kristina likes to have this privelege of seeing her oldest son at times too. The children are always welcome home to their humble abode. Neighbors are welcome too, as Laura always makes plenty.

Laura Kristina has made plenty of Swedish limpa rye bread for all the four hungry men who have come home for lunch. She also has some fresh churned butter and home made cranberry preserves (lingon). She was happy she had picked the lingon berries last Fall in the woods behind their house and made lots of lingon preserves. Klas loved lingon on everything!

Klas, Ole, Georg, and Nils Lennart were always ready for Laura's yummy meals. Klas bowed his head, folded his hands and thanked the good Lord for this fine meal that Laura had prepared for them.

Laura, as most mothers, cannot believe how quickly her youngest, Nils, has grown up to be such a fine young handsome man. He certainly takes after his dad. She knows he's leaving soon for the United States of America. She will really miss him, but she is ready for him to spread his wings and grow. She and Klas have had a full life rearing their four children. Laura wonders back to April 4, 1903, when her last child was born in Skogslund (the family farm name). He was a small baby, but he didn't stay that way long. He was always adventurous and ready for a new occurrence. He did all the risky things boys like to try and his fun was filled with sledding, skiing, and hanging out with his village friend, Gideon Wännerstam. Everyone called him "Bror", which actually means "brother". Laura then remembered to a time when Nils' big dog pulled him around the yard in his little wooden wagon. Wow how time does fly by! Nils and his Dad never liked farming. Nils would just as soon putter around in his Dad's blacksmith shop and learn how to make things-just like his big brother, Georg, too.

The small village of Haurida had a Luthern Church in the center of town, and a little general store owned by the Thòrens with a couple of gas pumps, two little one-room school houses that housed first-third grades, and fourth-sixth grades. The single teachers lived in apartments above the school houses. There was a cemetery next to the church. The church bells sufficed for both the schools and the church.

Since there was an abundance of forests in the area, there was a saw mill as well. Otherwise, there wasn't much activity for the young people. Many had big ideas to spread their wings and go to the big cities or Universities in Lund or Uppsala. A few went to the service, which is what Nils had decided to do. He wanted to travel. His big sister, Helfrid, was always talking about the golden streets of America, but she was content to settle down and marry her nice young man, Sven Aaronsson.

Helfrid was the oldest sibling and she and Sven moved to Huskvarna where he worked in the Huskvarna factory where they make different yard machines. They had a four-apartment building within walking distance of the factory on a pie-shaped corner lot. Helfrid and Sven have used their farmer skills to plant many fruit trees and bushes and other tasty things. There is no lack of beautiful flowers. What a delight this bountiful yard is. They had some of the most beautiful enormous roses too. It even had a welcoming swing and a table and chairs for a charming enticing Swedish coffee party (Fica).Helfrid learned many baking skills from her mother, Laura Kristina as well. Her kitchen was much more modern than her Mother's with an electric stove, and refrigerator and running water. They even had an indoor bathroom. Thank goodness. She is so grateful for Sven's good management of their finances, so she can live in a bit of luxury compared to her parents.

Klas & Laura Sandberg lived in the small village of Haurida about twenty American (three Swedish miles) east of Huskvarna and Jönköping. When they went to town with the horse and buggy, it was a long all- day excursion.

She cleaned the luncheon dishes and realized that women's work is never done. Soon it would be time to start kväl's mat (supper-the evening meal). She knew how much her fellows loved, fried smelts, and buttered, parsleyed new red potatoes, so she visualized how she would put together one of Nils' favorite suppers before he left. She wanted him to have a fond memory of his last days at home in Haurida with his family.

She was so happy she had taken the time yesterday to stop at the local village fish market to pick up the smelts and some fresh herring. She always made her own pickled herring.

She also had stopped at the village Thòren's general store and picked up some spenat (spinach) and lök (onions). She had everything she needed to make her special supper. She made creamed, sweetened spinach along with the smelts, new potatoes and fresh limpa. If she has time, she may even bake a socker kaka (sugar cake) for dessert.

She would finish the woolen undershirt after supper with the help of the light from the pretty turquoise flowered oil lamp that Nils used to do his school lessons by. Since it was winter, the sky grew dark around two-thirty in the afternoon.

Nils Lennart in the Swedish Royal Navy

Chapter 3

NILS' ADVENTURES

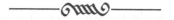

In 1924, Nils Lennart left for the Navy and Laura Kristina tried to acclimate herself to his leaving. Nils (Nisse, as was his nickname) liked the idea of adventure, as he had grown up moving around a bit from Haurida, to Vireda, briefly in Huskvarna, and back to Haurida where his folks finally settled back at Skogslund Farm. It was surrounded by lush green forests, where they could pick berries, mushrooms and lots of wild flowers.

The neighbors didn't live too close to each other. She got to see her neighbor, Mrs. Gustafson, occasionally around the bend and another neighbor when she went after milk on the bicycle.

She used her husband's bike so it was a little difficult cause he had such long legs and hers were so short. That was down the road in the other direction and it was a nice little outing for her. She would sing as she road along, and wave at the cows chewing their cuds in the meadow. It was a pretty ride.

The good-bye was a bit difficult, but Klas and Laura said their good-byes as Georg drove Nisse to the bus to take him to his Navy position. Laura wrote to Nils as often as she could, because she really missed him more than she thought she would. After all, that was her baby.

When he had almost completed his time in the Navy, he received a letter from an older Swedish cousin who lived in America, saying he would be glad to sponsor him and send him a ticket to come to the United States of America, if he so desired. One had to have a clean bill of health, have no criminal charges against them, and had to have a responsible adult party (preferably a relative) to sponsor them.

He had to ask permission from the King of Sweden to be allowed to get out of the Navy a little early to go. After receiving his release, and the ticket from his cousin, Carl Carlson, in Lafayette, Indiana, he was ready to go.

Mamma Laura Kristina Elisabeth worried about her youngest child leaving the nest in Sweden to go to the land of opportunity to the golden streets of America. He is my last child am I ready to let go of him? It was one thing to see him enter the Royal Swedish Navy. It is another to see him leave the Navy to go to the United States of America. So many gangsters!

Since Nils was leaving in January, 1926, his Mother knew it would be very cold aboard the ship and the cold Atlantic waters at that time of year. It took nearly a month to cross the ocean then. So, as a good mother, she knitted him a wool undershirt to wear on the cold crossing.

Once again, Klas and Laura said there goodbyes before he left for Guthenberg (Göteborg) to get his Swedish/ American Line ship called the Drottningholm. The seas were pretty rough that time of year, so it was a welcomed arrival in New York City in early February.

In 1926, immigrants were docking and coming into Ellis Island. This chilly February morning as the sparkling rays of sun bounced off the waves, Nils viewed the most beautiful sight of the large Freedom Lady, the Statue of Liberty. It gave him the most magnificent feeling of awe. It was a beautiful symbol of liberal living. This was what Nils Lennart Patrick Sandberg had come to America for. Freedom! Freedom to expand his desires to grow and succeed in a new adventure.

His big sister, Helfrid, spoke of it often enough for him to yearn for life in the land of golden streets.

He would now be able to pursue his dreams and wishes with a new beginning. A bigger country with lots of opportunities and big cities. He was the only one in the Sandberg family to ever want to venture to the U.S.A.

He thought maybe he could use some skills he learned in his father's blacksmith shop making tools or working in a manufacturing company. He liked using his hands and figuring things out.

He did not like farming at all, but wanted to create things. His brother, Georg, made lots of things and had dreams of building a stainless steel machine that would wash the dishes.

MOM'S MODEL T FORD & NILS 1927
DAD'S NASH MAY 15, 1958
HELEN MOM'S MODEL A FORD 1929

18

— *Chapter 4* —

THE WONDER OF TODAY'S MANFACTURING

Today's manufacturing has come so far, and one of today's manufacturing giants was forty when Nils was born and sixty-three when Nils came to the U.S. in 1926.

This marvelous magnate was Henry Ford and he founded the Ford Motor Company in 1903, the year that my dad was born. Mr. Ford established "Greenfield Village" in Dearborn, Michigan as a museum of things of the past that he liked to collect. It represented an early American Village depicting earlier characters such as Luther Burbank, Noah Webster, and others. It had an 1880"s machine shop, a replica of Edison's Illuminating Company where Ford had worked for years as Chief Engineer. There also was a white farm house duplicating the Ford Family farmhouse, a backyard shop where Ford had built his first horseless carriage in 1896 (the quadricycle).

There is also a replica of the first Ford Motor Company factory from 1903. It was the year that divided the American past from the American future. In his musem, he paid homage to men he admired like blacksmiths, machinists, and farmers.

After the war, in 1919, America had emerged as the richest and most powerful country on earth. American mass production on an assembly line, was instituted by Ford, and now had become the envy and admiration of the world.

Ford had become the first billionaire. In 1924, he also built the first all-metal tri-motorized airplane.

The press called 1923 the "Ford Craze" and the admiring fans looked on the Motor King as a benefactor.

This was a tremendous inspiration to many, including my father. The Model T had taken up half the roads. By 1926, the year my father came to the U.S., the Model T had essentially been un-changed since 1908. Ford assumed that Americans would want a Model T forever since it was durable, dependable, and simple. in fact, it was my mother's first car and Nils was excited to get to drive it.

Then Chevrolet drew Ford's customers a-way and automobile competition began. Ford decided to put the Model T out of production in 1927. Thus came the Model A. Mom got one of those too, which Nils wrecked.

In 1920-1929 America was in the postwar Depression while many were out of work; but Nils always managed to have a job due to his perseverance and persistence and positivity. Nils desired the idea of manufacturing in the New World too and became a fine toolmaker in Chicago, Rockford, Detroit, and Lafayette, In. He, as Ford, had no desire for farming. They both detested it.

LAURA KRISTINA & KLAS SANDBERG @ SKOGSLUND-1930
HAURIDA, SWEDEN
EDIT, HELGA, KLAS, MARILYN, HELEN & LEONARD-1946
1947, ULLA SANDBERG & RALPH
HELEN AND LEONARD, 1933
GOOD-BYE!

NEW YORK CITY PIER
MARILYN AND DADDY- 1946
1946- HELEN SANDBERG
ON-BOARD SWEDISH/AMERICAN
LINE DROTTNINGHOLM 1947

Chapter 5

MORE OF NILS' ADVENTURES

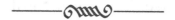

Back to 1926, when Nils traveled to America, the passengers had to hurry to this Ferrier that would take them to Ellis Island to be checked in. Once they got to the two large halls there were two very long lines where doctors were checking them one at a time. First, papers had to be filled out, but it was difficult to know exactly what they wanted, because Nils could not read English, and there were no interpreters on the island.

Nils had stood all day in the long hot line and he had started to itch and scratch under his arms until it was very red and irritated. By the time he got up to the doctor, he was very concerned at the doctor's intent, look and shaking of his head. He sent Nils to another room where he was held overnight. After this disgusting long wait, Nils decided they would probably send him back home on the next ship and he didn't even care anymore. He thought it might be better to just go home. He couldn't understand anyone.

He was tired and hungry. In a few minutes, a Swedish nurse from the ship came into the room along with the doctor. She looked at Nils and his rash was gone. After talking to Nils she found out his woolen undershirt had made him itch and Nils had scratched it the day before. The next day it was gone and once the reason was explained, and Nils did not have some contagious disease, they all had a good laugh.

Besides the difficulties of a long ocean crossing, Nils was beginning to realize there could be many more problems for a foreigner.

Nils deracinated himself from Sweden in 1926 to find a better life for himself. However, this uprooting was not necessarily easy by any means. There was no English language class taught in Swedish schools in those days as there are now, so Nils decided if he was going to make something of himself or even make it at all, he would have to work hard to learn this new language.

After all was approved, Nils was led to the bus station to take the long two-day trip from New York to Lafayette, Indiana where his cousin Carl and Eleanor Carlson lived.

February was cold here too-just like Sweden. This bus ride was grueling and tiresome and when he arrived, he was starving. Carl met Nils at the bus station and the town was a lot smaller than the bustling streets of New York where there were street cars, some horseless carriages and lots of horse-drawn buggies.

Eleanor, Carl's wife, met them at the door, and could tell Nils was exhausted, but before she offered him a bed, she asked if he was hungry.

Being the polite Swedish boy he had always been taught to be, he refused anything and said, "Oh nej tack." (Oh, no thanks). She asked how the trip went and when he yawned, she said "We can talk tomorrow. Are you sure I can't get you something to eat?" Well, Nils said when repeating the story later, that a polite Swede always waits for a third offer before accepting anything.

When the third offer never came, he went to bed starving and almost bent over in pain from hunger. He realized he was in a different country now and decided never to refuse something he wanted or needed again if it was offered to him. He learned to speak up for himself and not to be so shy any more.

After a wonderful night's sleep, Nils awakened to the smell of eggs and bacon cooking and good strong coffee brewing.

After a full tummy, he was happy to bring greetings from his mother Laura Kristina Elisabeth and dad Klas Magnus Sandberg to Swedish-American cousins, the Carlsons.

Laura Kristina had sent a hand woven Swedish table covering to Eleanor. It had beautiful interwoven threads of blue. Klas sent a hand carved wooden Dalar Horse from Dalarna to Carl.

They came in many different colors, but he had chosen a bright orange color. There was rosmaling flowers painted on the saddle area. The Carlsons were thrilled to receive something from their former home.

Carl took Nils around the neighborhood and showed him where he was a caretaker for the large estate and yard of a prominent man in town at Earlhurst.

On Sunday, Carl and Eleanor took Nils to the old Swedish Mission Covenant church where they attended at 16th and Grove streets. The minister preached in English, but Nils was glad to hear as much English as he could. After all, he needed to learn as soon as he could.

Chapter 6

LANGUAGE LESSONS & THE SWANSON FAMILY

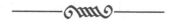

Eleanor started his lessons almost right away —every evening after supper they spent at least one to two hours with her pushing and drilling him. He was a fast learner though and it pleased them both. He learned phrases and questions to ask potential bosses.

He started working in the factory making tools rather quickly. Nils picked things up in a hurry. To his delighted surprise, he met a nice Swedish-speaking family at church by the name of Swanson. They had three boys and two girls. The youngest girl, Helen, was close to his age and played the organ. While she was born in Lafayette, she still knew how to speak Swedish and had even taken her Confirmation in Swedish from a Swedish minister who traveled between the country church, and Attica, and their town church in Lafayette to preach alternating days.

Helen was a pretty little twenty-one year old, while he was twenty-three. He began spending a considerable amount of time at the Swanson home. Helen had an older sister, Sylvia, who was twelve years older than Helen and was already married to David Gustafson. They had a farm out by West Point, not far from Lafayette. The family all called her Sis. Many of the Swedes who settled in the area were farmers.

Helen's dad, Algot Swanson, came from Sweden near where Nils' family had lived when he was only seventeen. He had been a tenent farmer close to West Pont working for several farmers before moving to town. His wife, Selma, came from Sweden with her family when she was only three. Some of her family settled in Kansas City while others went further west to Colorado and Seattle, Washington.

Algot had brothers in Rockford, Illinois. Helen had three brothers, two older, Stephen and Paul and her youngest was Kenneth. Stephen married Veva Gustafson, and Paul was married to Mary. Neither of those brothers ever had children. The youngest was married to Elizabeth Smith and they had four children (Gladys, Lorretta, Carol & Roger). Kenneth became a Covenant Minister studying at North Park Seminary, our Covenant denominational Seminary in Chicago.

He was the only sibling of Helen's to go to college.

After visiting the Swanson home so much, Nils became sweet on Helen and they started to date.

Eleanor told Nils that "Nils" was not a very Americanized name and if he wanted to fit in better, perhaps he should convert his Swedish "Lennart" name to the American version "Leonard". So, Nils, wanting to fit in, did just that and became Leonard.

Chapter 7

A LITTLE HISTORY OF THE ERA & LESSONS LEARNED

Calvin Coolidge was the 30th president during the time that Leonard came to the U.S.A. in 1926. Herbert Hoover became President in 1929. in March of 1929 the stock market collapsed.

Leonard never accepted failure and constantly approached life with a positive attitude.

What a gift! While there were a few who maintained riches, he definitely was not one of them.

He just was willing to plug along and learned how to be frugal. During the Depression he was never without work, because he Persevered and Persisted. This truly amazed me as so many failed and were without jobs and went hungry.

My father taught me lessons of how to persevere and push forward to accomplish your goal I think without him even realizing it. I recognized it in him, by the way he lived and responded and by what he accomplished. I believe as the youngest sibling of the family, he got lots of encouragement to venture out. He always had confidence in himself to accomplish anything he attemped to do. I saw that kind of confidence as well in my youngest child. She succeeded with great achievements as well even without college.

In fact, the other three of my children went to college and all succeeded.

He took a bit of a chance when he was asked by a potential boss if he could do welding. He had done very little in his father's shop, but felt very sure he could learn more on the job and do a good job as he progressed and went along. He was hired, and his boss realized he didn't know that job as well as he thought, but he was so im pressed with his perseverance and tenacity to practice and learn to do better, that he kept him.

Dad did learn in a quick fashion and he learned it well, because he had faith in himself.

My cousin, Michael told me a story recently about Dad that I had never heard before.

He said Leonard watched professionals work, and felt he could do the job just by watching them.

Dad had been watching these fellows lay bricks one day, and the boss asked, "Can you lay bricks?" He replied, with enthusiasm, "Sure, I can do that!" And low and behold he got the job. As I mentioned before, Leonard always had a job during the Depression, because he was willing to try anything.

I actually adopted this procedure when I interviewed for a job and knew I would learn and teach myself on the job as I had had to do on my previous job and because I knew my desire to persevere. I spent hours in the evening at home teaching myself how to operate an adding machine without looking. I learned it so well that I became one of the fastest most accurate keyers in the Accounting Department. We must condition ourselves to do well by practicing and believing in ourselves. When you key thousands of numbers without looking at your keyboard, you're bound to make a few errors in a month. I had a few months when I didn't even have one error or perhaps just one or two errors. My boss was very pleased with my performance.

Another valuable lesson I learned from my dad taught me the value of honesty. One day we had been to the drugstore and when he got two cents too much in change, he made a point to take it back to the clerk and had me go along.

That left an impression on me.

Chapter 8

PLACES LEONARD WORKED & MARRIAGE TO HELEN

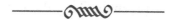

After dating Helen for a while, Leonard went to work in Rockford, Ill. as a toolmaker during the Depression where he met Anna Roselle. She was a Swedish girl who had come from Mönsterås, Sweden and was working as a domestic housekeeper for a family there. She ended up marrying Charles Wallgren. They settled down in Jamestown, New York, and had one daughter, Doris. Leonard always exchanged Christmas cards with the Wallgrens, so they never lost touch.

Leonard's toolmaking skills increased as he worked from 1926-1933 at Ross Gear in Lafayette, In., Rockford, Ill., Chicago, Ill. andDetroit, Mi. In 1928 he had saved enough to go home and visit his parents and siblings, but he contracted Scarlet Fever, and almost died. It took all his savings to pay the doctors back. He said he felt he was saved in Rockford by his landlady bringing him soup as he lay near to death. Consequently, Leonard never got to see his mother again since he left in 1926, and she passed away of Uterine Cancer in 1931. Doctors knew very little about cancer then and could do nothing for her.

Leonard had a chance for a job back in Lafayette, so he started dating Helen again.

They became engaged in 1933, but he wanted to visit home again one more time. He had already lost his mother in 1931, without getting to see her after leaving, so he wanted to make sure he could see his Dad. He managed to save enough for passage again, and he didn't want to lose the chance to go.

While he was there, he decided to attend Business College wanting to better himself. He ended up staying for two years. He was getting lonesome, so he met a family friend and got a little too friendly and she became pregnant. They did not want to get married, but she had a boyfriend who wanted to marry her anyway. He raised the girl, Anna as his own. She never knew who her real father was until her Mother was on her deathbed. The daughter eventually came to Indiana to meet her real dad, Leonard Sandberg. She had been working in Florida as a nanny for a lady for several years. Leonard's grown children never knew anything about her either.

When Ralph & Marilyn learned they had a half sister in Sweden, they were delighted and met her later at Leonard and his second wife's house in Lafayette. It was a lovely meeting and they have all kept in contact ever since. I don't believe Helen ever knew about her or I'm sure she would have told Leonard to marry the lady.

By 1935, since Helen and Leonard had been engaged for two years, Helen was concerned at getting older. She wrote to Leonard and Helen said, "If you want to stay in Sweden, that's fine, but if you still want to get married, and have a family, then we probably need to do It now before I'm too old to have children."

They got married June 29, 1935 in Lafayette, In. at Helen's folks' house on Alabama St. Rev. Paul Westburg, who came in 1933 to start up the church again after it had been closed down for two years during "slim times", married them.

6-29-1935 HELEN AND LEONARD SANDBERG WEDDING
LAFAYETTE, IND.

Marilyn, 1944
1936 Helen and Leonard
1938 Ralph and Daddy
Dad's Car 1943 & Dad

Chapter 9

FAMILY LIFE IN PEORIA, ILLINOIS

Helen and Leonard started their married life in a new town where Leonard had been offered a good job at the Caterpillar Company in Peoria, Illinois.

They found a lovely two-story family home on Armstrong in which to hopefully rear their future family. They had an elementary school a couple of blocks away and the neighborhood proved to be full of lovely families.

Ralph came along in January, 1937 and Marilyn followed in August of 1940.

Helen was happy to get to know a neighbor, Dorothy down on the corner who had two daughters-Edna and Judy. They both had afflictions and Helen was able to assist her occasionally. She had another neighbor in the next block, Alice, who also became close. In fact when Helen had her convulsions while she was in labor with Marilyn, Alice told her later that she owed her a new nightgown. When she heard the ambulance sirens coming for Helen, she panicked and her nightie got caught in the ringer of her washing machine and got torn to shreds.

The previous week the Sandberg family had decided to go on a little camping vacation In early August before the baby was due in September. However, Helen caught a cold, and the doctor gave her some cold medicine that did not agree with her. Since she didn't feel well, she went to bed a little early.

The next morning, Leonard told her to stay in bed and he would go down to start the coffee and make a little breakfast for Helen and Ralph. She really started to feel bad and yelled for Leonard and then passed out. He took two steps at a time and ran upstairs to the bedroom. He could not find Helen, but finally found her wedged between the wall and the bed on the floor. She had passed out. He got her up on the bed where she had another convulsion, so he ran to call the doctor and the ambulance.

When they got to the hospital, the doctor said she had Eclampsia, which was very dangerous then and still is today. Many times he said they usually have trouble saving both the mother and the baby, so he asked him, "Which do you want me to save?" He frantically cried, "Both!" This baby was a whole month early, so it was going to be difficult. However, miraculously, the doctor was able to save them both. They had to use forcepts to help get this little girl out and it bruised her left earlobe. Since she was a preemie they put her in an incubator to warm her. In 1940, the incubators were heated by a light bulb. They laid her near the lightbulb that made her earlobe turn black and scabbed.

Consequently, her earlobe fell off. People were not so sue-happy then as they are now. They were just happy to have her alive as well as her mother.

Since Leonard was a Shriner, they decided to take her to Shriner's Children's Hospital in Chicago where they performed three plastic surgery operations on her in her first year. They didn't know a whole lot about plastic surgery yet, so they did a kind of a botched up job. It was just lucky she was a girl and could wear her hair long to cover up her ear. She never got to wear pigtails or ponytails in her hair.

Leonard worked at Caterpillar for almost eleven years. Ralph went to White School in Peoria for Kindergarten through third grade and Marilyn just went there for Kindergarten.

White School used to have some wonderful carnivals. They had a cake walk and Ralph seemed to be very lucky. He had won two cakes in a row, and his teacher jokingly said, "Ralph, Why don't you win me a cake too?' Well, by gum, he did. He won a third cake! Who would have known?

The WWII had been going on, and people had problems getting nylon hose, coffee, sugar, amongst other items. We had to have coupons to buy things. We had a big block of white lard looking stuff they called margarine and we had to mix an orange capsule with it to make it look like butter. That was always my job. I remember sending coffee and hose to Sweden during the war cause they couldn't get any. The hose were actually made from silk.

Franklin D. Roosevelt was president in 1945 and died unexpectedly on 4-12-45, and Vice President Harry Truman became our thirty-third president. On August 6, 1945 he approved the dropping of the Atom bomb on Hiroshima, Japan.

Three days later, on August 9, 1945, a bomb was dropped on Nagasaki, Japan, and Japan surrendered on 8-14-1945, and WWII was over. The very sad thing was that people were vaporized. Usually really bad things happen even to end other bad things.

Truman's presidency also saw the founding of the United Nations. He also fought communism.

Truman was not always greatly liked or even appreciated,

however, my father felt he was one of our greatest presidents. The folks sold their house on Armstrong,and Leonard wanted to take his whole family to

Sweden to meet his Dad, and his other relatives and show them where he had come from and to teach them about his culture and traditions.I remember Mother sitting and crying as she put our school drawings and papers in the open furnace door.

Two of the few possessions she brought with her were her miniature Singer sewing machine and her big brown warm fur coat. I'm sure there were more treasures, but those two stood out in my mind. Even though we traveled by ship, space was limited as to what we could take.

The war ended in August, 1945, and we left for Europe in the Spring of 1946. Since it was so soon after the war was over, it could possibly be a bit precarious and dangerous. There have been a few places in the world that didn't get the immediate information that the war was actually over.

Chapter 10

THE 1946 FAMILY TRIP TO SWEDEN

It took ten long days to cross the Atlantic back then and we encountered some rough weather, and poor mother suffered terribly with seasickness and could hardly eat.

Perhaps some fresh air might have helped, but she didn't feel well enough to even be out of bed. She was happy to set feet on solid ground in Göteborg (Guthenberg). She lost quite a bit of weight from the trip.

Leonard's nephew, Conrad Sandberg, and Majbritt met them at the pier and took them to Huskvarna. They then stayed with Leonard's dad, Klas, in Haurida.

They met many relatives from all over the country throughout 1946. The children went to school in the Haurida village. Ralph to fourth grade and Marilyn to first grade in the two different one-room school houses.

Marilyn's best friend in Sweden in first grade was a little Finnish girl, named Perico that stayed with Grandpa's neighbors, the Gustafsons. She stayed for a year during the war. Many Finnish children stayed with Swedish families during the war so as to keep them safe. Finland was involved in the war while Sweden was not and had remained neutral. While we went to a little one room school house that held first through third grades in Haurida, Sweden, we were the only two foreigners in our class. She went back home to her parents a year after the war. I often wonder where she is now or if she's even still living. Who would have known over fifty years later that my son would become a post high school teacher in Finland teaching English as a second language for a year and a half. Funny how things go around in life.

My experience in grade school in Sweden was much better than my brother, Ralph's. I had a lovely teacher named, Betty Berring, and she knew a little bit of English and made me feel especially loved. Usually children don't start first grade in Sweden until they are seven and they didn't have kindergarten. Since I had been to kindergarten for a year in the States, and had interacted with other children, I was allowed to go to first grade in Sweden at age six. They said if she doesn't do well, she can always take first grade over again in America. Well, I fooled them! I not only learned Swedish, I passed all my subjects with flying colors, my Mom & teacher said.

I learned math on an abacus (which is pretty cool) and I haven't seen one since. I learned to write fancy cursive writing that they taught in Sweden and other things.

On the other hand, my brother went into the other one-room school house into fourth grade with a male teacher who ended up being brutal to my brother for some reason. He must not have liked foreigners – or at least Americans. The teacher instructed the other boys (some one and two years older) in the classroom to pick on Ralph.

When our father found out, he was extremely irrate and approached the teacher. Our father said, "My son is no more foreign than you. he was born of two Swedish parents and I personally originally came from this village. He apologized and began to treat Ralph a little bit better, but he never was very kind to Ralph. Thus, poor Ralph had a bit of a difficulty learning very much Swedish or gaining very many guy friends. However, the girls were pretty nice to him. After all, he was a real cutie.

It snowed a great deal that winter, and Ralph and I skiied often to school, which was about two American miles away on country roads. Since my skis were smaller, a local villager had made my skis. We used to hand wax them to make them go faster. We also had a sparkster, which was a chair-like seat on long runners, that the whole family would ride on. Mom would sit, I in her lap, and Ralph and Dad would stand behind the seat on the runners. We would rip down the hilly roads lickety-split. Lots of fun. I haven't seen one since either there or here, but I do think they still make them.

Ralph loved to ski, and one winter day he went out to the woods around Grandpa's (FarFar's) farm area, and got lost. The woods (skog) looks a great deal alike and it can be very confusing, and it's easy to get lost. He was out all day and he began to be a bit frightened. When the sun started to go down, he realized his directions and established which direction was North. He went until he reached a fence and then followed the road to home. Our parents were happy to see him approaching, but didn't completely realize his dilema until he reached home and told of his excursion. Guess all the Sandberg males liked exciting expeditions.

Ralph was a typical boy and loved to tease his little sister and her beloved cat, Sippa.

When all the snow melted in the forest, it made a big lake, and Ralph picked my Sippa up and flung her out into the middle of the lake. I was so upset, but my cat was extremely smart and strong.

Many a cat would have drowned, but not my Sippa. She surprised us all and swam right back to me. Ha! Fooled ya! Guess cats do have many lives.

One day when we had been gone all day, Sippa came in from outside and she had been attacked by another animal who had bitten a hole in her abdomen. She came into the kitchen meowing rather mournfully, and Mother said, "Ralph, are you tormenting Marilyn's cat again?" He said, "No, Mother, I haven't touched her." She went over to Mother, layed on her back and showed Mother her stomach. Mother couldn't believe how smart she was. She tried to clean her wound, but a cat and dog have healing properties in their saliva and she pretty much healed herself by licking all around her wound. And in a few days she was better!

The winter snow in Sweden was magical and so beautiful. The shower of feathery flakes made for a picture perfect enough for a postcard.

The white fluff clung to the naked limbs adding an atmosphere of heavenly peace. This was enchantment. Night time in the country brought a glowing starlight that one can't usually see in the city. It's an amazing show of lights in the winter.

However, in the summertime, one can read a newspaper at night outside, and it's what we call the land of the midnight sun.

After a year full of new exciting experiences the Sandberg family made it back to the states. they stopped in Brooklyn, New York, to visit Leonard's friend Bror and Elsie Wannerstam.

Marilyn got so excited to get to learn how to blow bubblegum bubbles from Elsie's sister. It is crazy the little things we remember you learned at age seven. Soon after they moved to Hollywood, Florida, where we visited them later.

SWEDISH SCHOOL, HAURIDA SWEDEN

SKOLA OCH LÄRARE I HAURIDA

Ralph was the 2nd from the right in the top row

MOM'S FUR COAT
HAURIDA
MOM & MARILYN
DAD, RALPH AND MARILYN ON N.Y.C.
GRANDPA'S BLACKSMITH SHOP
THE BLACK SMITH SHOP BURNED DOWN – NEW ONE BUILT

1950 IN USA
KLAS SANDBERG
ROCKEFELLER CENTER
New York City

ALGOT SWANSON'S GROCERY ON ALABAMA ST.
1940's

Chapter 11

BACK HOME AGAIN IN INDIANA & WHITE COTTAGE DAYS

Aunt Veva and Uncle Steve, Helen's brother, thought it was so cute and unusual to hear Ralph and Marilyn speaking fluent Swedish a blue streak.

Foreign languages are easy for children to learn, but if you don't keep it up, you can lose it as we did. The family then settled in Lafayette, Indiana, Helen's hometown, where her father still lived. Her mother, Selma, had passed in 1943. Helen's two brothers, Stephen & Paul and their wives also lived there along with her older sister, Sylvia, so they had family there. Brother Kenneth and family lived in Chicago, as he was a Covenant pastor there, and they were very close.

In 1947, the Sandbergs bought a home on Center Street, just three blocks from Helen's dad.Ralph and Marilyn spent the rest of their school years in Lafayette and both graduated from Jefferson High School. They both attended their denominational church college, North Park College in Chicago, Il.

In 1953 the folks bought the White Cottage Restaurant along

with a Standard filling station at the corner of South St. and U.S. 52 by-pass. Ralph and Daddy ran the station and Ralph was seventeen, and I was thirteen but worked hard helping Mother in the restaurant.

Highway 52 was the main corridor leading to highway 41 to Chicago from Indianapolis which went right through Lafayette, Indiana. This was before they built the major I65 highway (North and South) to Chicago from Indianapolis, the capitol of Indiana. We got lots of traffic and our folks made a go of the business where a lot had failed before. I was not a stranger to hard work at thirteen. My jobs had been tough enough as a babysitter. Especially to a family with three children, one being only a six-week old baby that I cared so diligently for. I kept the children clean and fed and even cleaned her messy house. I honestly think I did a better job than the mother. Maybe she was just tired. I dropped that job when I started helping my Mom.

It seemed easy when my mom had me waiting tables and peeling a big barrel of potatoes. I peeled until my fingers had blisters. My Dad paid me thirty-five cents an hour, the same as I got for babysitting. It wasn't a whole lot even then at thirteen, but I was happy to help out the family. We had hired some help both in the filling station and in the restaurant, but it was sad to see how good help was hard to find and even worse to see how they would steal from us when we weren't around. So we did as much of the work ourselves as we could. My brother worked just as hard helping our Dad pump gas and washing car windows.

There was a little old man that lived near by in a trailer and he would come over every day for my Mom's good bean soup. Many times she would just give it to him and not charge him for it.

I think that was when coffee was just ten cents a cup. I use to have a traveling salesman come through occasionally and he would always leave me a fifty cent tip. I thought I was in heaven since that was more than I made in an hour.

What a nice guy, I thought.

One Christmas Eve we decided, as a family, to give a gift to the Holiday travelers on US highway 52. We stayed open to accommodate them and many stopped saying it was the only place open between Chicago and Indianapolis. There weren't any fast food places back then—mostly mom and pop establishments and even the bigger restaurants were closed for Christmas Eve and Christmas day. I think we stayed open until midnight, as travelers kept stopping. One family came in exhausted, as it was a three-hour drive from Chicago to Lafayette. They got gas, shook off the snow, and blessed us for being open and feeding them. One gal was so famished, she ordered a dozen eggs. My Mom said she only had nine left. Her family said, "Oh, just give her three. She doesn't need that much!" We all had a laugh over that; she got filled up with bacon, toast, the three eggs, juice, and coffee. They were the last customers of the evening. We will remember the joy we brought to many that Christmas Eve as we filled their car tanks and stomachs.

In the restaurant, we had a juke box that played vinyls, and one time we came to the restaurant and there was a little mouse in the juke box sitting on a vinyl record. My brother got so excited, he wanted to catch it and make it his pet mother objected, of course, at his desire to bring it home with him, but he finally persuaded her. It got out of the box at home and ran into the pantry. He had me guarding the door out with a towel. I sat there quite a while as he searched for it until I got tired of waiting. That little bugger was quicker than an eye blink. None of us saw it trying to escape.

However, when I stood up, there he was squished by my knee. Ralph was so mad at me. Ha! Mom was actually relieved. She didn't want that little rodent loose in her house. End of that story. Stick to your dog, Trixie, as a pet, Ralph!

We all worked hard and it paid off. Our family was the first owners to make a profit for a long time, so we felt it was all worth it. Our Dad decided to sell it after a year and that's when he wanted to take Ralph on a trip to Sweden with him. Since Ralph had a girlfriend, he did not want to go. I really wanted to go, so Dad said, "Okay, you can go with me." Mother and Ralph stayed home and Mother got a secretarial job with the construction company that was going to build the new city sewage treatment plant. It was a good job for her.

WHITE COTTAGE RESTAURANT &
STANDARD FILLING STATION 1953
1947-1962
1418 CENTER FAMILY HOME
CHRISTMAS 1954
SANDBERG FAMILY

Chapter 12

LEONARD & MARILYN"S 1954 TRIP TO SWEDEN

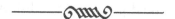

Daddy and I spent about four months in Sweden from April to August, 1954. Since I had forgotten most of my Swedish from early childhood, it was a magnificent chance for me to regain the knowledge of the Swedish language. I listened, I asked questions, I repeated and practiced. I was kind of shy, but I was anxious to learn.

Before we left America, I had to do some extra homework, but my principal felt this trip would be more educational than if I stayed home in school for two more months.

Being with foreign folks is the best way to learn a foreign language. I had an insatiable curiosity how to say everything and so I learned a great deal that summer.

I had learned my Swedish quite well at age six, in 1946, but then forgot it because I didn't use it anymore. My folks spoke very little at home and only when they didn't want us to know what they were discussing. I can attest to the fact that living amongst the people and being young is the best way to learn a foreign language. However, if you are out of that environment and don't use or hear it any more, you can forget it pretty quick too. One has to be interested, listen, ask questions, pay attention, and ask how to say something and then practice it. We perhaps only went to Sweden every seven or eight years and then fifteen, so we only got to observe and practice it then. I finally took Swedish in college for two years where I learned to read, write and spell it.

As you may know, it's difficult to learn much of a foreign language in a class room situation. However, I was very interested, paid better attention and truly tried to learn enough to use. These few times I went (now seven), I learned more each time. If I didn't remember how to say something, I would go to my Swedish/American dictionary to try to say and spell words correctly. I continue to write Swedish letters to my cousins and I call and talk to them on the phone. I would sometimes jot down what I was going to say ahead of time so I wouldn't sound too dumb.

They are amazed at how much I can speak, because cousins my age can't speak English. Most of the young people can because they have to take six years of English in school now. I do have one younger cousin who was a college professor at Lund University, and he speaks perfect English.

Language is not the only thing I learned. I learned a lot of what my mother had to learn in 1946. I drew water from the well, carried it to the boiling pot in the smoke house, heated and carried it back to the wash tub in the yard, scrubbed our clothes on a scrub board, split wood, we planted and harvested potatoes, put hay up to dry and I even raised a chick to hen-size to see her lay her first egg. To iron daddy's shirts, I even heated the old cast iron iron on the wood-burning stove.

Even though they stayed most of the time In the country at Leonard's father's still primitive home in the village of Haurida, Marilyn was happy to learn all these menial chores. Marilyn felt that these experiences would be remembered and treasured forever. Her dad was very proud of her and all she had learned. She felt like a pioneer. It was also fun to go see all their relatives in town. They visited Leonard's nephew, Conrad, and his wife, Majbritt, and their family and Faster (Aunt) Helfrid and Farbror (Uncle) Sven and their daughters, Gullan and Ingrid. And, of course, there was dear Uncle Georg (George) and Faster (Aunt) Edit and their son Stig. So many cousins! Conrad was interesting as he had a photographer shop in town and a band that went around playing music all over, including the park. He wanted me to sing with them one night, and I really wanted to, but I was way too shy to do that, so I said,

"No."

When we were in the country, I would ride Farfar's (grandpa's) bike down to the next farm to get the milk, just like grandma used to do. Since I did love to sing, I would sometimes stop in the meadow and sing to the top of my lungs. I didn't think the cows would mind. They just looked at me when I sang "Once I had a secret love." It was popular in 1954.

TRIPS TO SWEDEN

HAURIDA
1954
ONE OF LEN & ANNA'S MANY TRIPS TO SWEDEN 1970
HUSKVARNA 1960
MORA CLOCK AND MARILYN

Chapter 13

BACK HOME

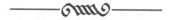

In 1955, Ralph graduated from High School and went off to North Park College in Chicago, Illinois.

Daddy took many jobs to keep the family afloat. He sold Filter Queen vacuums and air filters for a while. He was a good salesman, and he really proved that when he became an entrepreneurial sales person at the Sears and Roebuck farm store in downtown Lafayette. After he did well in the store, he presented a different idea for selling for them. He offered to go out to the farmers to sell them lightening rods for their barns instead of waiting for them to come into the store. It was a completely new concept to

The company, but they liked Leonard's enthusiasm and decided to let him try it. He became an even more successful salesman for Sears and he had the top sales.

Mother even rented out one of our bedrooms to a roomer at a time when things were a little sparse.

Daddy was always thinking and one day he realized he knew a lot about machining and the tool business. He even knew how to read intricate blueprints. He decided to go into business for himself as a middle man for companies who needed parts and things made. He knew what companies could do what and he started to travel around the country to get the idea rolling and to let the companies know that he could expedite the process for them by getting certain companies to make whatever they needed. He would assist in getting car parts and plane parts and many other types of manufacturing. He only asked for a 5% commission for being the middle man. Pretty soon he began to get many jobs to get quoted for the participating companies. in the beginning, he was on the road a lot, but eventually they trusted him so much, that they just sent him jobs to be quoted by mail. It became a fairly lucrative job for him and he even trained a couple of guys how to do it and they also made a good living for themselves and their families. I remember one job was to make man hole covers for a large city North of here. He called his company- Sandberg Engineering Manufacturing Company and he was a manufacturer's representative. Way to start your own business, dad and succeed in the New World after all! Your mamma Laura Kristina would have been proud of her little Nils. Klas was. Mother Helen became dad's proud, proficient, helpful secretary, and helped him a great deal. He worked this job until he was in his late seventies and then dwindled off since he didn't have mom to help anymore. However, I wrote a few letters for him as he dictated later.

Then in 1957, Ralph went off to the Army and went several places, but ended up in Taiwan and met and married his wife, Kathryn Huang in Taiwan in 1961.

Little Jacqueline Grace became Leonard and Helen's first grandchild in 1962. They became house parents to eleven girls, so it was almost like Jackie had eleven big sisters. They lived in Chicago, Illinois, and later started a Real Estate office.

In 1960, Marilyn graduated from North Park College in Chicago.

JEFFERSON HIGH SCHOOL 1958
NFC GRADUATION 1960
DAD-MARILYN-MOM

OUR PETS

1941
DIXIE or (BROWNIE) IN PEORIA
THE DOG
TRIXIE 1955
IN LAFAYETTE RALPH'S DOG
MARILYN'S KITTIES
1950
RUFFY; TUFFY; & FLUFFY

Chapter 14

THE 1960 TRIP TO EUROPE- FIRST BY PLANE FOR HELEN, LEONARD & MARILYN

Helen and Leonard decided to go to Sweden again and took Marilyn with them as a graduation present. She mentioned to them it was a shame to go that far and not go visit some other countries while they were there, as it was as easy as going like from state to state in America. They agreed, so they visited Norway, Denmark, Holland Belgium, The Netherlands, Germany, France, and changed planes is Great Britain and Greenland, and so they set foot in ten countries. They took lots of pictures and gathered many memories.

We were all glad for those experiences.

EIFFEL TOWER
PARIS, FRANCE
LONDON, SWEDEN PEOPLE'S CHURCH
HOLLAND WINDMILL
GERMAN GRASS ROOF

Dad, the businessman in his office

SANDBERG ENGINEERING COMPANY

Manufacturers' Representative

Production Machining • Welding • Chuckers Up to 30"
Tool and Die Work • Aircraft and Industrial Engineering and Machining
Gear Cutting • Special Machines Built • Stampings • Hydroforming
Screw Machine Work, All Secondary Operations
Castings of All Kinds • Zinc and Aluminum Diecasting • Forgings
Fasteners • Plastic Parts and Molds • Cold Heading • Springs

LEONARD SANDBERG

114 DIGBY ROAD
LAFAYETTE, INDIANA 47905
PH. 317-742-7489

*Dad at a factory making a contact, and his business
card as a Manufacturer's Representative for Sandberg
Engineering Manufacturing Company.*

Chapter 15

THE FAMILY GREW

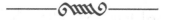

In mid July, 1962, Helen & Leonard moved into their new house on Digby Road, Lafayette, In.

In just two weeks after that Marilyn married her high school sweetheart, Leon Fleeger, in early August, 1962. They had four children. Since Leon was in the Navy, Annette was born in San Diego, Ca. When Leon got out of the Navy, they settled in Chicago and Marilyn got her job back at GMAC. Jeffrey was born in Chicago in 1966. Mother never got to meet the next two grandchildren, as she passed of a heart attack at age 63 in 1969. She had been visiting us in Chicago for a church conference that was being held at North Park College.

She did not feel well that last day and was anxious to get home to Lafayette. A few minutes after they left our apartment, Dad called with the shocking news that he felt Mom was gone. He was calling from a South side Chicago hospital, to say they were there. As soon as we settled our two kids with the neighbor friend, we took off for the hospital.

The next four days were very hard for all of us, and we knew Dad was very lonesome, so Kathy and I hired a live-in house keeper for him. We got an old friend who had been married to dad's cousin and was now alone, so it was a perfect fit. He felt comfortable having her there since he knew her.

Pretty soon he got in contact with his ole Swedish friend, Anna Wahlgren, from Jamestown, New York, in 1970 and came to find out she had lost her husband, Charles, too in 1969.

1969 was a memorable, historic year. Nixon was president, and the Apollo 11 landed on the moon. Mother never got to hear that news as she had passed June 18th, 1969. She would have been so thrilled for them. It was a memorable moment when Neil Armstrong, Buzz Aldrin and Michael Collins were the navigators.

A year after Mother passed, we realized dad was lonesome, so we decided to move back to Lafayette to be near him. We got the opportunity to buy our old home place on Center Street, which was just two and a half blocks from Dad. We did this in 1970, and Leon got a chance to start working in the Plumbers group with his brother, Don, and I got a job in the Accounting Department at Purdue University.

In the past four years, I had had three miscarriages, so I wasn't sure I could have any more children even though the doctor said I was fine.

I felt something was causing it.

I became pregnant again in January of 1971 and found an old-fashioned Obstetrician who seemed to know why I was having miscarriages at three to five months. He said my uterus was tipped, and once the weight of the fetus increased, the uterus just couldn't hold it, so it tipped out the fetus. All it took, was an exercise to do twice a day to put it back in position. Bravo so cheap and so easy to fix. All those fancy specialists in Chicago and Lafayette didn't know this simple explanation. So in the middle of September, 1971, I had my third child—my first miracle baby, Kristina Amelia Elisabeth, named after Daddy's mother. Then two years to the day, I had my second miracle baby, fourth child, Jennifer Helen (after Leon's mother and my mother) Michelle. We finally got our four children we wanted.

Since Dad had kept in contact with Anna that he had known in Rockford, but now lived in Jamestown, he found out that she had lost her husband, Charles, too in 1969. They got back together again and married in August, 1970, on my birthday. They were very happy to find each other again.

Anna had a bit of a different personality than my Mom. But she could be lots of fun. She was a good Swedish cook too, and was always up for a get-together, as are most Swedes. Dad always wanted company over. Dad went to New York to help Ann sell her house, and she moved across country to begin her new married life to Len, as she called him. Boy, can you imagine all the name changes this man has gone through!

They had lots of fun revisiting Sweden, their homeland, over the next few years. Annette was seven, and Jeff was four and a half, when they married, and Kristina and Jennifer never knew anyone as a maternal grandma except grandma Ann. She had us for meals, Christmas gatherings and lots of coffee parties. She was willing to babysit my children if I needed her to. In turn, I would have the family for Thanksgiving get togethers.

LEONARD AND HELEN-1969

Chapter 16

DAD & ANN'S FINAL SWEDISH CHRISTMAS TRIP WITH MARILYN IN 1992

The folks always wanted to go to Sweden in the spring or summertime. However, we got to talking about how much fun it had been to be in Sweden during Christmastime, so we made plans to go one more time at Christmas. We had our immediate family Christmas celebration at Thanksgiving. I put my Christmas tree up for Thanksgiving and we celebrated both that year together in 1992. We went ten days before Christmas to Sweden and had planned to come home the day after.

We had lots of fun going to relatives and seeing all the cousins again. We had rented an apartment in the center of Huskvarna as well as a car. We even drove down to Lund and stayed with Helfrid's daughter, Gullan and saw her son Magnus & Monica and their family. Of course we spent Christmas eve at Lasse's for dop I gryttan (dip bread in the pot of broth), and then evening fest (kalas) with lots of smörgåsbord food at Conrad and Majbritt's. The children anxiously awaited the Jul Tompte's (Santa's) coming. Santa comes and knocks on the door and asks if there are any good boys and girls here? Majbritt put poems on all her Christmas packages.

After supper and gift exchanges, our friend, Karl Frederick came by to have coffee with us. He knew we were going home in another day. Dad had gotten back from the bathroom and started to slur his words and couldn't pick up his coffee cup. My cousin, Susanne, felt he was having a stroke, so they called an ambulance immediately. We followed it to the hospital.

Dad not only had a stroke, but a heart attack as well. He had severe blockage in both carotid arteries. He ended up staying in the hospital and nursing home for six weeks before being allowed to come home. I was in contact in Sweden every day with the doctor. The only way he would let him come home was if we hired a nurse to come with him and Ann and buy her a round trip ticket.

When he got to Chicago, we had to get him an ambulance from the airport to Lafayette Home Hospital. He got to see Ralph, my husband Gene, me and the grandchildren. He was happy to be home in the States. He only lasted three days, and he got to be burried next to his first wife, our mother.

*114 DIGBY SANDBERG HOME 1962-1992 LAFAYETTE
ANNA & LEN 1984*

ANNETTE 1963 KRISTINA *Her chap* JENNIFER
DAVE JEFF JOHN *16* BOB *24*

Annette & Dave, Jeff, Tina & John & Jen & Bob

Chapter 17

FINAL TIME WITH ANN

Ann stayed in the house for eight months, as dad had arranged for her. Ann was ninety by then, and wanted to move back to Jamestown to be close to her daughter, Doris. She lived to be ninety-seven. She was in a nursing home the last few months, but was failing. Doris said she just wanted to talk Swedish and no one could understand her. So Gene and I felt we should go see her and I could talk to her which she loved.

By 1992, Anna had started to have memory problems. In the Fall of 1992, she was blaming Marilyn a great deal for taking her things. Marilyn kept trying to help the folks with all they needed. Dad had Marilyn writing his checks and helping him as a P.O.A. (power of attorney) to take care of his business deals. Ann never wanted any of that help from her. Her dementia caused her to assume that the things she put away were disappearing by someone else. She had always had a kind of jealous feeling toward me because Daddy and I had a very close association. So when she hid things, she forgot and felt she had to blame me for taking them. It hurt me so very much, but perhaps I was hurt more than I should have been. At the time I did not know about Alzheimer's. I just thought she hated me, and I was really hurt. She told the ladies at church that I was terrible and was stealing from her. I would never take anything from her or anyone that didn't belong to me. She was very convincing and said, "God knows I don't lie!" I was further hurt when I felt I was being shunned by the ladies and surprised they would believe her after they had known me all my life.

Years later when I experienced Alzheimer's firsthand by taking care of my Alzheimer's husband for eleven years, I figured it out and realized that that was what she was going through. Had I known then, I could have saved myself all that grief.

One day when I came over, she said her beloved shawl that her sister had sent her from Sweden was missing. I felt for her and offered to help her look for it. We looked and looked all over for it, and couldn't find it, much to my dismay. Several days went by and one day I came by, and Anna had her shawl on her shoulders. I said, "Oh, good, you found your shawl!" "Oh, sure, " she said. "It's because you brought it back!" I was stunned. No, I had not brought it back, because I never had had it!

It was further crushing when I felt my brother had not been by my side. He said later, he had been, but I never heard it. He was hurt because he thought I would know he stuck up for me. His silence to me made me assume he believed I was at fault. It caused us unnecessary discord. I felt dejected that he didn't speak up for me TO me. He said, "How do you know I didn't stand up for you?" I said, "Maybe you did, but I never heard it" . Words between us could have alleviated all of this, and we both could have been relieved of all this heartache. I ended up writing a poem concerning this anguish. We were separated and not speaking for nearly six months. Our family had always solved any disagreements quickly before. It just goes to show you how important it is to communicate with each other. Do not let time pass.

I did not understand at the time that this was probably dementia causing Mother Ann to act this way. I still loved her, and forgave her, but was terribly hurt thinking it was all due to her deciding to dislike me. It was about ten years after her passing that I truly understood dementia. There are many valuable lessons we can learn in life on a daily basis.

Daddy felt so lucky to have been married to two wonderful Swedish ladies. He said the good Lord really blessed me. And we were all Blessed by having each other in a loving Swedish family.

MIDSUMMER POLE JUNE
SANTA LUCIA PARTY – MARILYN
12-13-1980
A SWEDISH COFFEE- PARTY-FICA

Printed in the United States
By Bookmasters